The Science of Bespoke Living

DESIGN YOUR IDEAL LIFE
AND LIVE IT NOW!

The Science of Bespoke Living

DESIGN YOUR IDEAL LIFE
AND LIVE IT NOW!

Wayne Malcolm

WAYNE MALCOLM INTERNATIONAL

Malcolm, Wayne

The Science of Bespoke Living: Design Your Ideal Life and Live It Now!/Wayne Malcolm

ISBN: 0-9543937-0-8

Printed in the United Kingdom
Published by Wayne Malcolm International

How to Order:
Single copies may be ordered from Wayne Malcolm International, P O Box 24532, London, England E17 6WZ; Tel: 08708 40 56 40. Quantity discounts are also available. On your letterhead, include information concerning the intended use of the books and the number of books you wish to purchase.

Visit us online at **www.waynemalcolm.com**

Wayne Malcolm - In Person

As one of the UK's most dynamic speakers, Wayne Malcolm speaks annually to audiences ranging from civic and church groups to business forums and sales organisations. In addition to this, he travels extensively with his Designer Life Workshop sharing the principles and technologies contained in this book.

If you would like to experience Wayne Malcolm in person at your event, log on to **www.waynemalcolm.com** and follow the instructions on screen. A complete schedule of his itinerary and life-enhancing products are also available online.

Contents

Dedication

I dedicate this book to all those people who dream of a better life. We all have dreams but often they seem so distant and unrealistic that the pain of pursuing them outweighs the pain of staying put. Staying put is a tragedy because it robs the rest of us of your greatness. Yes, your success would no doubt impact the rest of us and make the world a better place. The good news is that your dreams are not as distant and unrealistic as they seem. WithThe Science of Bespoke Living you can design your own future and then step right into it. God put those dreams in you because they depict your destiny. You could technically do anything if you knew what to do and then did what you knew. I pray that when you finish reading this book, you will know what to do.

Wayne Malcolm

Acknowledgments

I wish to thank my family and staff for releasing me from my regular duties and keeping my life together whilst I absconded to write this book. Many thanks!

Introduction

THE WORD *'SCIENCE'* means knowledge. It assumes that the universe as we see it is really a set of effects originating from a set of causes. Science says that there are no effects without causes, and that if a cause can be discovered and understood then one may use it to create an effect, should that effect be desired. This law of cause and effect underscores all aspects of scientific research and is the sovereign rational behind every aspect of our existence. The Bible says it this way: *'Whatsoever a man soweth, that shall he also reap.'* His circumstances and conditions, whether good or bad, are effects for which there are definite causes. To change the effect, he must first change the cause.

The word *'bespoke'* means customised, tailored, made to measure or personalised. It is usually used in connection with clothes or shoes. A bespoke suit is created to fit the body and suit the tastes of the person for whom it was specifically made. Bespoke shoes are created to fit the feet and suit the tastes of the person for whom they were specifically made. In the same manner, a bespoke life is created to fit the destiny and suit the needs of the person for whom it was specifically made.

Now, just imagine that five years from now your life is absolutely ideal and perfect in every way. What does it look like? Spiritually, physically, socially and financially - what does it look like? Your family, your friends, your career - what does it look like? Whatever you are seeing in your mind's eye right now is an effect for which there are definite causes. If you can discover those causes, you can use them to create that effect much sooner than you think. The science of bespoke living is about how to harness the power of proven causes to create the desired effect of a successful and fulfilling future.

There are only two ways that you can live out the rest of your life - by design or by default! When word processing on a computer you have the privilege of customising your documents to suit your own tastes, requirements and needs. If you fail to do this, the computer's own default setting will determine the look of your document for you. The same is true in life. You have the option to customise your life to suit your own tastes, needs and dreams. Any failure to do so will subject you to life's own default setting. Unfortunately, the default setting for life is **REPETITION**, i.e. the circular motion of coming back to square one and to that all-familiar feeling of *'I have been here before' and 'Here we go again.'* You are literally doomed to repeat until the day you design! The choice is simple: customise your life or accept life's default setting.

Guilty of Doing Nothing!

A ***judgement by default*** is a judgement passed in favour of the plaintiff when the defendant fails to appear in court or to enter a plea. The same is true in life. Any failure to design your future will result in a ***life by default,*** which is effectively a judgement in favour of your past and against your passion!

There are five basic reasons why most people will never design their future:

1. **They Are Too Busy** - Most people are caught up in the survival **SIN-drome** where most of their mental and physical energy is spent making it, coping, bearing up or surviving. Such people are too busy

making a living to think seriously about designing a life.

2. **They Don't Know What They Want** - Some people have allowed their past to obscure their true passion so much that they have completely lost touch with who they really are and what they really want.

3. **They Don't Know How To** - We've got designer clothes, jewels, cars and homes, but no one ever told us how to design a life! Learning to drive is compulsory, whilst learning to live remains optional. Consequently, most of us don't know how to control the outcomes of each day, month and year.

4. **They Don't Believe It's Possible To Live Their Dreams** - Finding fulfilment, living our dreams, and achieving our goals often seems way beyond our reach. However, the flags at the top of the summit stand as proof that this mountain is far from invincible. Everyone before you who made it to the top got there in exactly the same way - they took one step at a time!

5. **They Don't Believe That They Deserve A Great Future** - Such people are too busy mending the past to make good of the future. Whatever you can do to tie up yesterday's loose ends should be done without delay. However, there are some things you cannot change or undo. You must accept this and move on. Stop punishing yourself for your mistakes, foolish decisions and bad behaviour. Learn from it and move on.

The Good News!

Most people are wearing a life that was handed down from parents, siblings or society. It was probably bought off the rack and was no doubt mass-produced to fit all shapes and sizes. Worse yet, there are those whose life is like a school uniform. It is a life of both conformity and obscurity where they are not allowed to stand out, be different, or otherwise express their individuality.

Most of us shop in the same sorts of places, live in the same sorts of houses, drive the same sorts of cars, and recreate in the same sorts of ways. However, there is an elite group who do not. These are the individuals who practise exclusive living. These insist on exclusive clothes, cars, homes, holidays and jewels, all uniquely tailored to their own personal tastes. Of course, these people can afford to sport their exclusive collections as status symbols and trophies of achievement. Most people cannot afford to do this and if they could, the rich would do something else because being different and exclusive is what they are all about. It is their unique ID.

You may not be able to afford the exclusive life or to design your own home, clothes, vehicles, holidays, workspace, jewels and furniture today. But the good news is that nothing at all prevents you from sitting down right now and designing the rest of your life. With a few simple skills and techniques you can design a life that glorifies God, fulfils you and positively impacts everyone and everything you care about.

What is the Designer Life System?

Most people are aware that something is missing in their lives but have attempted to fill the void with all sorts of square pegs that will never fit. Actually, the missing element for most of us is a life management system that delivers measurable results and regulates the outcome of each day, week, month and year. Without an effective system your life can spiral out of control leaving your defences high, your self-esteem low and your personal progress virtually non- existent.

The Designer Life System is an integrated personal manager for all the key aspects of your life including your time, money, health, relationships, career, projects and faith. It is designed to deliver measurable results in each of these areas and to create a pathway from where you have been to where you belong.

Are you ready? Then let's begin!

CHAPTER 1

Becoming Successful

Before You Succeed

'A life without cause
is a life without effect.'

Anonymous

CHAPTER 1

Becoming Successful

Before You Succeed

SUCCESS IS ACHIEVEMENT and therefore an effect for which there are definite causes. The use of a proven cause to create a desired effect is the essence and art of success on any level and in all areas. If you can determine the cause of a particular effect then you can use it to create that exact effect over and over again, whether that effect be a fit body, a happy home, entrepreneurial success or an athletic victory. If you can find the cause, you can create the effect.

The Causes of Success

Success is achieving your goals without violating your values, but **success-full-ness** is a state of mind or quality of thought. It means to possess those internal qualities that make success inevitable. The successful person is full of success.

All religions, philosophies and meta-physical studies agree that your mentality is magnetic and will attract the people, opportunities and resources necessary to manifest your predominant thoughts. This means that you will inevitably become what you think about most of the time. Your life will veer towards the dominant picture in your mind.

If your mind is full of success then you are successful and will inevitably succeed. Success is the effect; successfulness is the cause. You do not become successful when you achieve; you achieve when you become successful. You are not successful because you achieved; you achieved because you are successful. You do not succeed in order to become successful; you become successful in order to succeed.

You must first seek to develop the inner qualities that make success inevitable because these inner qualities are the causes of success. Success is an effect or a result. It is the result of being successful.

Because the law of cause and effect may be applied to success, it is safe to say that life is no respecter of persons and will deliver the same results to whoever will apply its timeless laws to their goals, irrespective of race, age, gender or religion.

Your thoughts are causes and your circumstances are effects. If you can discover what successful people think about most of the time and then do the same, you will have used a proven cause to create the desired effect of a successful and fulfilling life.

The Five Forces of Change

Successful people think about five things most of the time. The fact that their minds are full of these things is evident by their words and by their careful use of time. They are **dreams, faith, goals, strategies,** and **action**. I call them the Forces of Change. They are responsible for man's highest achievements. Every invention, advancement and accomplishment of mankind owes its existence to the dreams, faith, goals, strategies and consistent actions of courageous people. The aeroplane, the light bulb, the Internet, the sky scrappers and automobiles all owe their existence to these creative forces.

These five are the most effective tools for forging the future known to man. They each possess mysterious powers to create or destroy and as such should be handled with great care. If man's greatest achievements were made possible by these five forces, then you may utilise these to achieve your own personal goals or even to create your ideal world.

The Power of a Dream!

Your dreams are the graphic pictures of the things you deeply desire, produced by your creative imagination and previewed on the big screen of your mind. They emanate from your core desires and true passions, which in turn emanates from your true identity, i.e. the person you would be if all the limitations were taken away.

The use of your creative imagination to paint graphic pictures of the things you truly desire will activate the magnetic properties of your mentality and begin attracting the people, opportunities and resources necessary to manifest that picture.

You can activate this dream force by thinking seriously about the future. Think graphically and regularly about the things you truly desire. See them in your mind's eye and stay focused upon them.

When in motion, it is essential that you look where you are going because you will swerve in the direction of your focus. If you are walking north whilst looking west you will end up in north-west if not in west altogether. The same is true in life. Your life is in constant motion. The only thing that is certain about your life is that it is constantly changing. That is why you must use your mind's eye to look where you are going. If you focus upon your problems you will move towards them. If you focus upon your desires, you will move towards them.

When shooting, you are told to aim then fire. The only way to aim is to look steadfastly at your target. It would be folly and possible tragedy to fire at a target whilst looking at something else. The same is true in life; you get what you aim at. But you cannot aim at anything you are not focused on.

Thinking seriously, regularly and graphically about the things you desire will activate your innate dream force. Eventually, your subconscious mind will begin seeking for ways to bring your desires to pass. Ideas will spring up from nowhere, opportunities will be detected in an instant and significant people will suddenly show up.

You will eventually become whatever you are mindful of. Those mindful of the past are forever mending. Those mindful of the present are busy maintaining. Those mindful of the future are constantly moving forwards in the direction of their dreams. If you look back, you'll go back. If you look around, you'll go around. If you look forward, you'll go forward.

The Power of Faith!

Your personal philosophy is the greatest single factor influencing and controlling the outcomes of your life. What you believe about yourself, the future and life itself will determine how far you go along the pathway of success. Your beliefs and values may either propel or prohibit your potential. To activate your faith force you should identify those beliefs and values that are dis-empowering and self-limiting. They must quickly be replaced by an empowering and self-leveraging personal philosophy.

Your ideal future does not require the faith of anyone but yourself. Belief in the future is really a belief in yourself. If you do not believe in your future it is because you do not believe in yourself. Self-doubt is the opposite of self-confidence and comes from a distorted self-concept. A distorted self-concept is the mother of all disfunction. It gives birth to low self-esteem, fear of failure and rejection, lack of confidence, insecurity and the poorest quality of relationships. It is the arch-enemy of the achiever.

If you suffer from a dis-empowering self-concept, it is because of the conclusions you drew from the things that happened to you in the past. You cannot lay hold of the future until you let go of the past and the only way to let go of it is to reinterpret it.

You are not responsible for everything that happens to you in life but you are responsible for the meanings that you attach to those things. You should point blank refuse to attach negative meanings that depreciate you to the events of the past. Even the painful experiences served the purpose of educating, motivating, conditioning and positioning you for life-long success. The Bible says it this way: '...all things work together for good to them that love God...' It does not say that all things are good and pleasant but rather that they are useful and serve good purposes. The best way to activate your faith force is to belief in yourself.

Entrepreneurs know that every human need, no matter how small or great, presents a business opportunity. By creating a solution to that need a business is formed, people are employed and the economy gets stronger.

One man's personal philosophy interprets human need as a problem whilst another man's personal philosophy interprets the same as an opportunity. The one is a pessimist, the other an optimist. One gets frustrated whilst the other is elated. One gets bitter whilst the other gets better. The core difference between these two men is their personal philosophy.

The high achievers look for the opportunities that adversity brings. They believe in themselves and feel quite unstoppable in their passionate pursuit of a dream. They have embraced a personal philosophy that says if at first you don't succeed, try, try, try again. Sir Winston Churchill lead Great Britain to victory in the second world-war with a personal philosophy that said, 'Never give up!'

The Power of Goals!

Your dream only becomes your goal in the day that you decide to live it. A goal is anything you aim to achieve or intend to accomplish. The words 'aim' and 'intend' are designed to distinguish goals from wishes. Creating a wish list is not the same as setting goals. For a future experience to qualify as a goal, it must be something you aim to achieve or fully intend to accomplish. In the absence of a decision to pursue it your dream is nothing more than ambiguous wish that do not qualify as goal.

Your goals act like mind magnets in that they possess a degree of pulling power. The moment you establish a goal, your mind will immediately begin to figure out ways to achieve it. In this respect, the goal will pull you towards it. Your brain will literally begin seeking for the necessary information and power to achieve the goal. However, the more clarity and definition you give to your goal, the more pulling power it possesses.

For example, if you set a goal to lose weight, you will immediately become conscious of the foods you eat and the levels of physical exercise you enjoy. You may begin to cut down on fatty foods, drink more water, start walking, etc. Such is the pulling power of your goal.

However, if you set a goal to lose 16 lbs, you have given greater clarity and definition to your goal, thus increasing its pulling power. You will immediately purchase some bathroom scales and begin monitoring your weight loss. You will become more cautious of the foods you intake. You will notice the effect that certain foods have on your body. You may even purchase a book on the subject or participate actively in a weight loss programme.

If you go a step further and set the goal to lose 16 lbs in 2 months, you have given even greater clarity definition to your goal by attaching a deadline to it. You have now maximised its pulling power. You will automatically develop an intelligent plan to achieve your goal and monitor your progress rigorously, increasing your efforts as the time goes by.

If you go a step further and write down your specific goal, complete with your intelligent plan, and read it regularly, your weight loss is virtually guaranteed.

The failure to clarify a goal robs it of its magnetic properties and ultimately renders it powerless.

The moment your dream becomes your goal, you have effectively changed direction. You are now heading towards your dreams. You are on route from your current life-location to your future dream destination.

Your current life location describes your current circumstances and state of being on four levels, i.e. your spiritual, personal, social, and economic reality. It is where you are right now, as opposed to where you have come from or where you want to be and could otherwise be called your address. The good news is that your identity transcends your address. They are not one and the same. Where you are right now does not tell me who you are in reality.

Your dream destination describes where you want to go in terms of your personal state, circumstances, and lifestyle. In this respect, it is a wish and only becomes a goal in the day that you decide to pursue it.

Your direction describes the results that your daily habits, routines, and activities will produce. Direction is always linked to a result or outcome and can only be described in terms of one. If you are going in a positive direction, it means that your thoughts, actions, habits and routines will eventually produce a positive result. If you are going in a negative direction, it means that your thoughts, actions, habits and routines will eventually produce a negative result. Changing direction is a matter of making your dream your goal.

You cannot change your life location in one day, but you can change your direction immediately. To change direction, first establish a new destination, make a firm decision to pursue it, and start taking steps towards your goal.

Where you are right now is the result of a direction you have been moving in over a period of time. You simply took steps in that direction. Not only does this simplicity explain how you got where you are, it also explains how to get where you want to go. Both your life location and your dream destination are arrived at in exactly the same way - you take strategic steps in that direction!

The good news is that you can reach your dream destination much quicker than you did your current life location. The reason is that most of the steps you took to where you are were subconscious and inconsistent. When pursuing a dream, the entire process is accelerated because your steps become both conscious and consistent.

The Power of a Strategy!

'He who fails to plan, plans to fail!' Anonymous

Your strategy describes a sequence of activities designed to deliver the specific results you desire. It is your plan of action. It is the path or sequence of steps that leads directly to your desired results. The most effective strategy is an informed, complete and executed strategy.

An informed strategy is one that has been thoroughly researched and carefully constructed. A complete strategy is one that incorporates clearly defined outcomes, a precise sequence of steps, tasks or activities, a list of necessary resources including human, financial and technological requirements and finally some strategic deadlines for each step or phase in the plan. An executed strategy is the only one that works because it is the one that you work by taking action and follow through.

The Power of Consistent Action - Habit Force!

You may be dreaming right now about a successful future and may even believe in yourself enough to make that dream a personal goal. Perhaps you have gone a step further by developing a comprehensive strategy for achieving that goal. However, none of these things will deliver the results you desire until you take action. You must act, take the first step, start the ball rolling and go for it. Initially, taking action may seem difficult but if you can discipline yourself to follow through on your decisions you will quickly tap in to one of the most potent forces known to man - habit force!

Your habits are responsible for where you are today and are the only way to get to where you want to go in life. They are the daily steps that you take in either the right or wrong direction. Bad habits are really steps in the wrong direction and they lead to the wrong place. If you are in the wrong place today, it is because you took steps in the wrong direction. Those steps are your bad habits. If, on the other hand, you are in the right place, it is because you took steps in the right direction. Those steps are your good habits. In this respect, your quality of life is the result of your routine.

The little things add up and eventually become big helps or big hindrances to your personal progress. That is why if you are serious about changing your life, you must start with the root causes of your discontent, namely your bad habits. You can only change the big things in your life by changing the little things upon which they depend. So start with your habits.

The beautiful thing is that you can make or break any habit in the space of a month. Anything that you do consistently for 25-30 days will pass from the realm of conscious effort and into the realm of subconscious ease. Your early days of discipline will serve to program both body and mind for effortless repetition. Try it. Try getting up every morning at 5.30am. Do it consistently for 25 days using an alarm clock. Then on the 26th day, take away the alarm clock. You will find that your eyes open and you'll be wide awake at 5.30am on the dot because your body and mind would have been sufficiently programmed to do so.

You can break your bad personal, social and financial habits through just 25 days of conscious effort. You can also develop new personal, social and financial habits by doing the same.

Hopefully by now it has dawned on you that you have got what it takes to make your dreams come true. If you have a dream and the faith to make it a goal and the discipline to follow through on a well-constructed plan, then you have an unlimited supply of what it really takes to create your own future.

CHAPTER 2

Locating Your Passion

The Process of Self-Identification

'Hold fast to your dreams
for if dreams die, then life is
like a broken winged bird
that cannot fly.'

Anonymous

CHAPTER 2

Locating Your Passion

The Process of Self-Identification

HIGH ACHIEVERS POSSESS a powerful sense of identity. Within them resides an amazing sense of significance, worth and value. They know that they are special and feel capable of achieving on the highest levels. Low achievers, on the other hand, tend to possess a distorted self-perception and low self-esteem. Low self-esteem is the mother of all insecurities, fear and timidity. It paralyses your performance and cripples your competences. It is the result of a distorted self-concept and can only be overcome by a revelation of your true significance and value.

Those who suffer from a distorted self-concept tend to confuse their identity with their address. They think that where they are in life defines who they are in life. They allow the past and even their present circumstances to determine their worth in God's master plan. However, nothing could be further from the truth. Your passions describe who you are and your past simply describes where you have been.

What Is Your Passion?

Your passion is your true obsession. It is that which would make life worth living for you, and that which you would do if money were no obstacle and if the past hadn't obscured your future. The thing that you would most like to be remembered for by a future generation is your passion. Your passion should determine your future and not your past because it alone tells us who you really are.

Identifying Your Purpose And Passion

Your passion reveals the true you and tells us where you belong. It is the greatest single clue to your true identity and the driving force behind of your new Designer Life. You will never be able to identify your true passion in life until you can think without limits. There are four main limitations that obscure your true identity - your money, your time, your physical condition, and your level of knowledge. Most goal setting exercises still permit these factors to govern the goal so that you end up aiming for the things that you think you can afford or have time to do or are physically capable of achieving or that you know how to do.

Most of us don't think outside of this box and therefore never tap into our true passion. To find out who you really are, you have to look at what you would do if the money, your time and your physical condition were no obstacle. What you would do if you never had to work another day in your life? What you would do if you had the time to do it? What you would do if you knew how to do it? This is who you really are and the only reason why you are not that way right now is that you cannot afford it or you don't have time for it or you don't know how to.

We tend to play by the rules of the game without ever questioning those rules. Rather than limiting your dreams by these conditions and restrictions, you should make it your great goal to have the money, time, condition, and knowledge to do the things you really want to do.

Limitless thinking is a winning habit because it keeps you in touch with your true self and your deepest desires.

Your Personality

There are basically four personality types based on varying combinations of two particular character traits. These character traits have to do with how you communicate, whether directly or indirectly and whether you are task or people oriented. Direct or indirect communication + task or people orientation = one of four dominant personality types. You will fit into one of these groups as either a direct/task person, a direct/people person, an indirect/task person or an indirect/people person.

Why is this important? Because a lot of people find themselves in professions or relationships that do not suit their personality. A direct/task person might make a good group CEO. A direct/people person might make a great coach. An indirect/task person may make a great accountant or writer. An indirect/people person may make a great athlete, etc. (See the chart below). Its important that you understand your personality type and that you pursue careers and relationships that compliment your personality. Of course, we neither have the time nor space to fully explore the role that your personality plays in forming rich and fulfilling relationships but what is important is that you work with your personality and not against it by pursuing a career or a relationship that does not suit you. Enough said for now!

Your Dream Profile

If I asked you to tell me about yourself, you would immediately draw from the past. Your personal profile would depict your experiences to date. However, your past only tells me where you have been and not where you belong. So let's start by developing your dream profile because this will tell you where you belong?

Answer the 21 questions below and then use the answers to create your own dream profile.

Think Without Limits

What three things in life do you value the most?

Name 10 people you would want to contact with an 'I love you' message before you die.

Describe your ideal spiritual state.

In what subject would you like to be regarded an expert?

How far would you ideally take your education in this subject?

What is your ideal weight?

What sports do you wish you could do well?

What hobbies or recreation would you engage in if you had the time and money?

What is your basic personality type?

Would you continue working your job if you suddenly received £25 million?

What work would you do if you didn't need money?

How much money would you like to earn per month?

In what way would your physical appearance change if you had the money to dress as you like?

Where would you live if money were no obstacle?

How much travelling would you do if you have the time and money?

Name 10 places you would like to visit before you die.

Name 10 things you would like to experience in life before you die.

Which area of human need would you do something about if you had the time and money?

What would you do to make the world a better place if you had the time and money?

What one thing could you do, become or achieve in life that would give you a sense of total satisfaction?

For what would you most like to be remembered by a future generation?

My Dream Profile

My name is ______________________________

The three things I value most in life are

1______________________________

2______________________________

3______________________________

These three get the best part of my time and energy:

The most important people in my life are

1____

2____

3____

4____

5____

6____

7____

8____

9____

10_______________________________________

These are the people that I speak and listen to the most:

I am in good spiritual shape because I

____

____

____

____

I am in good mental shape because I am an expert in

____

____

____

____

and have taken my education ____________________ on this subject.

I am also physically fit in that I weigh ____________________ lbs, and have plenty of time for the recreations and relaxations that I enjoy namely

____

____

____

____

My basic personality type is

____,

which suits me for the work I do as a ____.

I do it because I love it and not for the money.
You see I already earn £ ______________________ per month from investments and live in ______________________. That is why when you see me, I look like ______________________ .I have been to many places including ____
____
____
and have done a lot of things including ____
____
____
____.
I really do feel for the people of the world who ______________________ and have supported their cause by ______________________________________.

My magnificent obsession in life is to
____
____
____
____.

If I can achieve this, I will literally die in peace and be remembered as the person who

____

____

____

____

The purpose of this exercise is to locate your passion and true purpose in life. This dream profile describes where you belong and should now become your grand objective in life. Having completed this exercise, you are now ready to develop a mission statement.

Your Mission

Based on your passion, you should develop your mission statement. Your mission is to pursue your passion by becoming the best that you can be at doing what you do. It is to live your dreams and thereby help others to live theirs. Your mission in life should become your focal point, your grand objective, your great goal and your overall purpose. Aim for it, and then fire!

Your mission should never be to do anything but rather to

become everything that you can be. Becoming something is more virtuous than doing something. If your mission is to do something great then you will spend most of your time working on it. But if it is to become something great then you will spend most your time working on yourself. If your mission is to do something great then when its done, your work is over. But if it is to become something great then your work never ceases. Becoming the best that you can be is not the same as becoming the best in the world. It is becoming the best that you can be which may be much better than the best in the world to date.

Document Your Destiny!

Your mission statement need only be one paragraph. State who you are and what your great goal in life is. Be passionate about your mission. Make it an imperative and explain a little about how you intend to pursue your passion.

'I am Wayne Malcolm and my true passion in life is people-building. My mission and overall purpose in life is to become the very best people-builder that I can be. By so doing, I will live my dreams and help many others to live

theirs too. I will pursue my passion through education and experience. I will speak, write, and record the life- building principles that work for me and thus make them available to the widest possible audience.'

Having developed a mission statement you can condense it into a slogan or an associative phrase. What do you want to be associated with?

'Wayne Malcolm - People-building at Its Best!

Once you have developed your mission statement and a personal slogan you are now ready develop your first five-year plan.

CHAPTER 3

Aiming to Live!

A Plan for Life

If a man does not know
what port he is steering for, no
wind is favourable to him.

Anonymous

CHAPTER 3

Aiming to Live!

A Plan for Life

THE AIM TO Live technology is fundamentally a goal setting exercise based on a five-year plan. It is unique in that it forces you to consider your life and future on four distinct levels.

Your life is more than your living; it encompasses your entire being. A life plan is more than a livelihood plan. Many people make the mistake of planning the future in financial terms only. For the most part, they are planning to make enough money to live their dreams. However, if your future plans are all financially driven you may make it in business but you'll lose it in life. You may make it at work but have to fake it at home. You may make lots of money but will lose the plot physically, mentally, socially and spiritually.

A financial plan is all about wealth creation. A health plan is all about wellness. A family plan is all about the quality of life at home. A faith plan is all about the depth of your spiritual life. However, a life plan takes all these into consideration and seeks to enhance the quality of your entire life experience. It looks at your very essence and adds value to every aspect of your existence.

When developing a life plan you should set goals in at least four areas of your life:

1. **Your Spiritual Life -** This includes feeding your faith, strengthening your beliefs, reinforcing your personal philosophy, connecting with God, fulfilling your purpose, giving, sharing and serving, prayer, worship, moral codes, and meditation. Each of these major contributors to the quality of your life experience should be factored in to your personal life plan.

2. **Your Personal Life -** I am now referring to your physical and mental well being as part of your overall development. It includes your health, hobbies, education, and relaxation.

3. **Your Social Life -** Here we consider your personal network of relationships including spouse, children, parents, siblings, extended family, friends, colleagues, acquaintances, customers and suppliers. Goals in this area are essential to the success of any life plan because quality relationships is the essence of success. Your personal network should grow in strength and number as the result of a definite plan to do so.

4. **Your Financial Life -** This includes your personal finances, wealth creation, business plans and financial security.

The Aim to Live Technology ensures that you set goals on each of these levels. That is why there are 4 rows in your aim to live chart.

Three Phases

Aim to Live is a five-year plan fulfilled in three phases. Why five years? Because five years is a realistic time frame for the creation of your new Designer Life! Remember, there is no such thing as an unrealistic goal, only unrealistic time frames. If you set a goal to be a billionaire, it is realistic if you are talking 25 years but unrealistic if you are talking next month.

Why three phases? Because every good story has its beginning, middle and ending! The three columns allow you to phase your plan into long-range, mid-range and short-range goals. The three columns and four rows of the Aim to Live system allow you 12 groups or categories of goals. For example, you may have mid-range personal goals or short-range financial goals or long-range social goals, etc.

So Where Do We Start?

Always start with your dream, i.e. your desired results. This is the master key to living by design. First, determine where you want to be, what you want to achieve and what you want to become on all four levels in five years time.

Aim *to* Live

1.	Long Range Question	Where do I want to be in 5 years time?
2.	Mid Range Question	What do I need to do consistently for 2-3 years to guarantee my outcome?
3.	Short Range Question	What can I do over the next 6 months to guarantee the start of phase two?

Range	Short : 6 mths - 1 Year	Medium : 1-3 Years	Long : 3-5 Years
Spiritual			
Personal			
Financial			
Social			

This column tells you what to aim for; it shows what you will become and it documents your dream! When planning your work, go from finish to start but when working your plan go from start to finish!

Where Next?

Continue working backwards and go straight to the mid-range column. This column no longer deals with where you want to be but rather with where you have to be in order to get where you want to be. On each level in this column you must describe the things you need to do consistently for three to four years in order to achieve your long-range goals, whether they be to study, to save, to practise, to take therapy, to cultivate habits or start companies. This column describes the things you will do to get the results you want.

And Then...

We have finally reached the starting point, which as far as planning goes, is the finishing point. In this column you should list all the things you need to do in order to make the second phase a reality. This means preparation. For six months to one year, you'll be getting information, making applications, enrolling, conducting research, tying up lose ends, setting things in order, bringing closure to conflicts and generally getting ready to take off.

Changing your life is like moving house. It is really a three-part process. After the logistical preparations, there comes the physical task of packing and loading up. After that, there is the journey and finally settling into a new and improved quality of life. The Aim to Live technique works in exactly the same way when working the plan. First, make logistic preparations and pack your bags for the move. Then, embark on the journey. Pursue your passions along a carefully chosen path. At the end of your path will be your dream destination! Enjoy it and then develop another five-year plan.

You can get to wherever you want to go in life in exactly the same way that you got to wherever you are right now. You took significant steps in that direction over a period of time. Now, if this policy got you where you are then it can get you where you want to go. Getting to where you want to go in life is as simple as taking significant and consistent steps in that direction.

Critical Success Factors

What if the list of things you need to do in the first phase is overwhelming and seems too much? The first thing to do is categorise your list. Group the goals together based on the things they have in common. Then employ the power of a focal point. Look for the links in each category by asking yourself, 'What one goal in this category, if achieved, would make everything else possible?' Or ask yourself, 'What is the most difficult or daunting task on my list?' Once you have the answer, you have probably found the one thing that links all the other tasks/goals together. If you can achieve it, the others will be as simple. If you climb this hurdle, the others will be nothing. Once you have found the link, then make it your critical success factor. Determine to achieve it first and by so doing you will guarantee the success of every other goal in that category.

CHAPTER 4

Shifting G.E.A.R.S

Accelerate Your Potential

No one can predict
to what heights you can soar;
even you will not know until
you spread your wings.

Anonymous

CHAPTER 4

Shifting G.E.A.R.S.

Accelerate Your Potential

GREAT GOALS ARE really a mosaic of smaller goals and tasks, which when achieved create the big picture that we call success. Your dreams for this year may only come true if you achieve your goals for this quarter. This will not happen unless you achieve your goals for this month. But these depend on your goals for this week and of course they rely on your goals for this day. In this respect, success is not a place as much as it is a journey. It is more of a direction than a destination.

For an athlete, success is not just winning the race; it is training, developing and practising for peak performance. When the race is won, it is only the evidence of his success. It is the proof that he practises, the test of his training and the demonstration of his athletic development. He wins on a daily basis by achieving his goals for that day.

Goal Orientation

The second exercise in this programme is a goal setting exercise based on a five-year plan. However, you don't have to wait five years to succeed. By designing your days, weeks and months you can experience the rhythm of success. By achieving daily, weekly and monthly goals, success will become a daily reality instead of a distant possibility.

The rhythm of success is an awesome experience. It occurs when the practise of constant goal setting passes from a discipline to a habit. It takes approximately 25 days for a discipline to become a habit. During this time your efforts pass from the conscious mind to the subconscious mind. They start out as conscious efforts but about 25 days later they become subconscious efforts. They start out difficult and uncomfortable but they become easy and comfortable. You can make or break any habit through 25 days of discipline.

When this principle is applied to the practice of goal setting, you become an unstoppable force and an immediate success because yours days, weeks and months become personal achievement zones.

Your five-year plan is a phased plan. You have long-range, mid-range and short-range goals. However, these goals may be broken down even further and advanced through 90-day increments. Ninety days is approximately three months and represents one quarter of the year. Your goals for any one-year may be phased in four quarters. In each quarter you have approximately 90 days to significantly advance your life plan. Remember, your five-year plan is an outline plan from which the true details are omitted. They could never fit into that little box. Advancing the plan will require detail in the form of a whole new set of goals that are necessary to achieve your major goals. It is as though each major goal is really a jigsaw puzzle made up of many other smaller goals, all of which must be achieved in order to realise the big picture. These smaller yet highly-significant goals may be advanced through 90-day increments.

Why 90 Days?

Because 90 days is a realistic time frame for making significant advances in your life plan. Any shorter is pushing it and creates pressure. Any longer is stretching it and creates apathy. Ninety days is just right for making significant changes to your life. In 90 days, you can lose weight, join a club, change jobs, read up to 12 books on a given subject, learn to drive, buy a home, create financial order, take lessons, start a course, cultivate new domestic habits, cultivate new social skills, develop any habit, break any habit, research thoroughly any subject, etc. In 90 days you can do it!

The 90-day Plan!

He who fails to plan, plans to fail. No business is worth investing in that doesn't have a written plan. The business plan is fundamental and essential to the success of any business venture. If this is true of business, what is true of your life? A life plan is fundamental and essential to the success of your life experience. Most people don't see it that way and that is why their plans, if any, are in their heads and not on paper. Documenting your decisions is a winning habit. Your five-year plan should be written and stored safely where it can be quickly retrieved and regularly reviewed. However, the success of this plan depends on the success of your 90-day increments. Every 90 days you are either progressing or digressing. To guarantee progress you should harness the power of a 90-day written plan.

Clear Goals, Clear Results!

The purpose of the Designer Life 90-day Planner is to clarify your goals and strategy for that period by documenting them using the G.E.A.R.S. technique. The clearer your goals, the more pulling power they possess. Remember, all goals possess magnetic properties, which act both internally and externally. Internally they pull creativity, invention, ingenuity, genius, and innovation out of you. Externally they attract opportunities, good people and material resources. Such is the power of goals. Clarify them and you will achieve them.

G.E.A.R.S.

G.E.A.R.S. is really a formula for results. It is based on a winning philosophy that says, 'All that stands between you and your dream is information and action.' You could technically achieve anything in life if you knew what to do and did what you knew. Those who fail in life either do not know what to do or do not do what they know. These two, knowledge and action, are like the oars on a rowing boat. One without the other produces a circular motion, but together they make progress. Knowing what to do is one half of achievement; doing what you know is the other.

Accelerate Your Potential By Changing G.E.A.R.S.

G **is for GOAL:** First, say in a nutshell what it is you want to achieve. This must be a one or two liner at the most. It should be your goal at a glance.

E **stands for EXPLORE:** You must now go and find out what to do. You should get information so that you can determine a more accurate course of action. This may be obtained from books, the

Internet, a mentor or simply by asking those who have achieved it already. Remember, knowing what to do is half the way to achieving your goal.

A **is for ACTION:** Now that you know what to do, you must take action and do what you know. Doing what you know is the other half of achieving your goal. Your research should result in a list of tasks, steps, or activities necessary to achieve your goal. This is your action plan. It should be broken down into definite steps. You can then use the **Making Progress** chart to determine deadlines for each step within your 90-day plan.

R **is for REASONS:** You should here state why you want to achieve this goal, what exactly is motivating you to achieve it, and how important it is to your overall life plan that you succeed.

S **is for SUCCESS:** In this section, write your desired outcomes as though they had already been achieved, e.g. I have lost 10lbs, I have saved £1000.00, or I have read 5 books on how to start a business, etc. This exercise not only serves to identify success when it comes but also to -

DLT-3: GEARS

Designer Life Technologies

Goals:

My **First Spiritual/Financial/Personal/Social** goal

____

____

____

Exploration:

I will get information about how to achieve my goal from the following sources:

Books ______________________________

Internet ______________________________

Mentor ______________________________

Questions ______________________________

By this date __________ I will have gotten the necessary information to determine a more accurate course of action.

Action:

I will take the following course of action to achieve my goal

Step 1 ______________________________

Step 2 ______________________________

Step 3 ______________________________

Step 4 ______________________________

Step 5 ______________________________

Step 6 ______________________________

Step 7 ______________________________

Reasons:

Why is this goal important to me?

____

____

____

____

1. Motivate you by helping you to idealise the goal, i.e. to feel the wonderful sensation of having achieved it;

2. Keep you focused on the bull's eye. Your focal point should always be your desired results. Activity is not the same as productivity. Knowing what to do is not your goal. Neither is doing what you know. Getting your desired results is your goal. Stay focused and get your results.

Conclusion

The shifting G.E.A.R.S. formula for achievement is to determine what you want, find out what to do, and then do what you know to get what you want.

CHAPTER 5

Designing Each Day!

The Power of Habit Force

There is no
giant step that does it.
It's a lot of little steps.

Peter A Cohen

CHAPTER 5

Designing Each Day!

The Power of Habit Force

THE MASTER KEY to success on any level is to develop one all-important habit - the habit of living by design. Customising your years, months and days through goal setting and time management is the most effective way to live out the rest of your life. Using the Aim to Live technique, you can successfully design your years. However, your years are made up of months, weeks and days all of which require strategic management.

Success is a journey, not a place. It is a direction, not a destination. You are succeeding so long as you are making consistent progress towards a personal ideal. In this respect, it is a daily thing. Every day provides an opportunity for success and for advancing your life plan. Every day that opportunity must be seized with passion. You should greet each new day with both gratitude and enthusiasm because it brings with it a world of possibilities. It brings with it the most valuable of all human commodities - time. Everything that you can be or achieve will be done in time. Without time you can become nothing, achieve nothing, and do nothing. With time on the other hand, you can become something, achieve anything and do everything you want to do.

The First Key to time management is to **re-evaluate time itself.** How valuable is your time? The people I meet seem to fall into two distinct categories - those who **have time** to waste and those who **have no time** to waste. Those who have time to waste *(The Time Wasters)* are that way because they have no goals. They have no purpose and therefore no passion. Those with no time to waste *(The Time Chasers)* are that way because they have goals and a passionate determination to achieve them. The basic rule is no goals, lots of time; lots of goals, no time. The moment you establish a goal, your time becomes that much more precious. This law applies to your years, months, weeks and days. It all becomes precious the moment you set a goal.

The value you place on time is always in direct proportion to the value you place on your goals. Time is only important if your goals are important. Time is only essential if your goals are essential. When re-evaluating time, make your time as precious as your goals.

The Second Key to time management is to **develop the habit of goal and result orientation.** Start everything with the end in view and start nothing until you know what it is you hope to achieve. From now on, everything in your life must start with targets, goals, objectives, desired outcomes or required results. Start each day with a clear mental picture of how you would like the day to turn out. Remember, if you aim at nothing specific in life, you hit your target every time. If somebody says, 'I want you to help me with this project,' your first question should be, 'What are the objectives of the project and what are the specific results you are looking for from me?' Before going to bed at night, you should take out a few minutes to determine your desired outcomes for the next day. That way you wake up in the morning mindful of your goals. 'If you don't know where you're going, you'll spend a long time on the road'.

The Third Key to effective time management is **the ability to discern a distraction.** Distractions come in many shapes and sizes but they come for the same reason and have the same effect - to break your focus and waste your time. Any unscheduled intrusion is a distraction. There is a difference between an obstruction and a distraction. An obstruction may require problem-solving skills, whilst a distraction will require the power of focus. Whenever you are in motion it is imperative that you look where you are going because you will swerve in the direction of your focus. If going north, look north. If you look west whilst going north you will end up in northwest. The same rule applies when focusing on a task. You cannot complete a task whilst focusing on something else. Completing tasks requires focus.

The temptation to multi-task is always there. However, working through your list of tasks and refusing to start the second until the first is completed has proven to be a more effective time saving technique. This is because it guarantees productivity. Multi-tasking guarantees activity, but it does not always deliver productivity. Working on a task does not make you productive but completing one.

The Fourth Key to effective time management is to **develop the art of time saving.** This means finding quicker ways of getting the same quality of result. This art is developed through keeping your work space tidy, delegating certain tasks, timing your calls, timing appointments, avoiding office chat, shorter lunch breaks, working whilst travelling using your mobile office (laptop or palm top computer), not accepting unscheduled appointments and many more.

The Fifth Key to effective time management is to cultivate the habit of thinking on paper. This means to work from a predetermined list of tasks. The difference between a task and a goal is that a task describes your activities whilst your goal describes your desired result. Your activities should produce a desired result. Your goals are your desired outcomes, whilst your tasks are the outputs necessary to achieve your desired outcomes. Your day must start with a list of things you have to do in order to get the list of things you want. Your question at night before you go to sleep should be, 'What do I have to do tomorrow to get what I want tomorrow?' Then, write it down as a list and work through it throughout the day.

The Sixth Key to effective time management is to **develop the habit of prioritising your tasks.** Of course, all your tasks are important, but some are more important than others. These are usually the ones that relate to your values and dreams, i.e. the things you personally value (family, faith, friends, future, finances) or the things you want to achieve. The important thing is to keep the important things important by doing the important things first.

The Seventh Key to effective time management is to **employ a daily formula that guarantees success.** A formula is a way of achieving the same result over and over again.

The Designer Life Formula is as follows: **Outlook + Input + Output = Outcomes.** The formula works like this:

1. **Desired Outcomes:** Always start your days with the end in view. Always start with your desired outcomes and personal ideals for that day. Describe what you want to achieve and how far along your pathway you want to progress. Write it down.

2. **Positive Outlook:** Nothing has more power to influence the outcomes of your life than your outlook in life. Your outlook is what you see when you look out. In a nutshell, it is your attitude! Your faith and focus, what you believe and expect out

of life. You must give time on a daily basis for feeding your faith, strengthening your beliefs, elevating your attitude and reinforcing your personal philosophy. This should be done as part of your daily success routine through prayer, affirmations, idealisation, reading, quotes and rehearsing your personal mission statements. Audio and video programmes, church and conferences, seminars and mastermind groups also contribute to a positive, healthy outlook. Write down exactly what it is you will do to feed your faith tomorrow.

3. **Quality Input:** Your body is like a motorcar. It needs fuel and oil to keep running effectively. The basic body fuels are nutrition, exercise and rest. These are not simply fuels for the body but they also contribute to a healthy state of mind, which in turn ensures peak performance and maximum achievement. You must design a day that allows for good eating, some cardiovascular exercise, e.g. walking, cycling, jogging, swimming, and some quality rest periods. Plan your meals, exercise and rest periods. NB: Just 20 minutes of pure, concentrated rest will do wonders in rejuvenating both body and mind.

4. **Consistent Output:** When planning the day most people think exclusively in terms of outputs, i.e. tasks, responsibilities and deadlines. They pay little or no attention to the physical and mental fuel necessary to secure a good outcome. Your outputs are most effective when you have first tuned the mind and body for optimal performance and maximum results. Make a clear list of all the things you have to do tomorrow in order to secure the results you desire. This list should only include those tasks that require personal output but do not fuel your personal engine.

The Final Key to effective time management is to **harness the power of TIMERGY. TIMERGY is my word for time and energy in the same space.** Often people give time to tasks but little energy. This occurs when multi-tasking or when distractions and interruptions arise. As a result, far too much time is spent on the task. This creates less time for other tasks, which in turn creates unnecessary stress. On the other hand, some people give lots of energy but little time to a task, perhaps through an over-ambitious attempt to accomplish too much in any one day. The result is usually a compromise on quality, a rushed job and high levels of exhaustion.

The answer is to balance your day between blocks of ordinary time and blocks of Timergy. Timergy is pure concentration. It is the art of being where you are, doing what you are doing and refusing to do anything else until what you are doing is done. It is refusing to take calls or interruptions or even to think about any other thing than the task or tasks at hand. Ordinary time is a little easier in that you may slow down your pace to do chores, make private calls, follow up or through on personal matters, return calls, send thank you notes, read papers and basically work on the less important things in life. The basic rule is that important tasks (including outlook and input related tasks) require Timergy. Not just time but time - energy.

How you balance your blocks of Timergy and ordinary time depends on what you are trying to achieve. Ordinary tasks require ordinary time. Extraordinary tasks require Timergy. You will achieve in two hours of Timergy what would normally take 3 hours of ordinary time.

Design *Your* Day

OUTCOMES:	OUTLOOK:
INPUT:	OUTPUT:

ADDITIONAL NOTES

CHAPTER 6

Making Progress

The Triple A Technique

Destiny is not a matter
of chance, it is a matter of choice.
It is not a thing to be waited for,
it is a thing to be achieved.'

William Jennings Bryan

CHAPTER 6

Making Progress

The Triple A Technique

You cannot make it without a journal. Don't challenge me on this just trust me on it. You say, 'I know someone who made it but doesn't keep a journal.' I say, what a waste! How can future generations benefit from their experiences? A personal journal is one of the most powerful tools in the hand of an achiever for the following reasons:

1. Any progress that cannot be measured cannot be

determined. You may be making progress or you may not; only the records can tell.

2. Without an accurate record of your daily activities, you may think you are making progress and are not. This inevitably leads to the frustration of disappointment, discouragement and disillusionment. On the other hand, you may think you are making no progress when actually you are. This, again, produces the same kind of frustration.

3. A journal is necessary to separate your feelings from the facts. Where you are externally and how you feel internally may be worlds apart. Controlling your feelings is the key to controlling your life. If your feelings are out of control then so is your life. The facts are the key to controlling your feelings.

4. There is just one way to control your feelings and that is to focus on the facts whilst interpreting those facts in your favour. You can focus on the Biblical facts, on the fact that you are a gifted person with a great future to seize, on the fact that a significant number of people love you, on the

fact that your past cannot defeat your passion, and on the facts of your journal. Your journal is a potent force because it contains the facts.

5. You can defeat frustration with the facts recorded in your journal. Your journal contains an accurate record of day-to-day activities, thoughts, experiences and emotions. If reviewed regularly, patterns can be identified along with strengths and weakness. Significant people, places and events will never be forgotten and the raw material of your future autobiography will be safely stored.

Perhaps the most important feature of your journal is that it allows you to activate The Triple A Technique for accelerating your dream. Triple A stands for Assessment, Adjustment and Acceleration. Every 30 days, you should use this technique to advance your 90-day plan and ultimately your destiny.

Why 30 Days?

There is a danger in practising The Triple A Technique too frequently. Some people prefer to conduct weekly assessments. However, tangible results may not be visible in one week. This inevitably leads to frustration. Likewise, too few assessments may reveal that a major adjustment to your plan was needed months ago or indeed that you are accelerating in the wrong direction. Thirty days is a realistic timeframe for monitoring your progress.

Of course, you can practise this technique weekly so long as you don't get frustrated with the seemingly negligible results.

How Long Does It Take?

The Triple A Technique may take anything from one to three hours and basically involves reading through every page of your journal and then using the information documented therein to answer some strategic questions.

The Personal Assessment!

Start by reading through your five-year plan, then your 90-day plan, and finally the previous 29 days of your journal.

The reason for this is that progress can only be measured in terms of a distance from your destination. You will have to work out whether or not you are any closer to achieving your goals. Your goals must be clear from the outset. Re-reading your five-year plan and your 90-day plan will mean that you are ready to assess your performance based on its relationship to your goals. Your goals must be the judge of your performance. High performance is achieving your goals; low performance is not achieving your goals. The question is, 'Where are you now compared to where you set out to be?'

When reading through your journal, look for good and bad patterns, strengths and weaknesses, helps and hindrances, joys and sorrows, as well as high and low performances. You should then answer the following questions:

What steps did you take this month towards achieving your spiritual goals?

Are you where you intended to be on this level at this time? YES/NO

If no, why?

Are there any problems to solve on this level?
YES/NO

If yes, what?

Have you discovered any habits to break or form on this level?

If so, what?

Did anything significant happen this month to either help or hinder your progress?

What have you learned about yourself in this area?

What can you do to improve your performance on this level?

What steps did you take this month towards achieving your personal goals?

Are you where you intended to be on this level at this time? YES/NO

If no, why?

Are there any problems to solve on this level?
YES/NO

If yes, what?

Have you discovered any habits to break or form on this level?

If so, what?

Did anything significant happen this month to either help or hinder your progress?

What have you learned about yourself in this area?

What can you do to improve your performance on this level?

What steps did you take this month towards achieving your social goals?

Are you where you intended to be on this level at this time? YES/NO

If no, why?

Are there any problems to solve on this level?

YES/NO

If yes, what?

Have you discovered any habits to break or form on this level?

If so, what?

Did anything significant happen this month to either help or hinder your progress?

What have you learned about yourself in this area?

What can you do to improve your performance on this level?

What steps did you take this month towards achieving your financial goals?

Are you where you intended to be on this level at this time? YES/NO

If no, why?

Are there any problems to solve on this level?
YES/NO

If yes, what?

Have you discovered any habits to break or form on this level?

If so, what?

Did anything significant happen this month to either help or hinder your progress?

What have you learned about yourself in this area?

What can you do to improve your performance on this level?

Honesty

The worst thing you could do with your journal is lie to yourself. You should be brutally honest when filling out your journal and when completing your self-assessment questions. It is the truth that sets you free. By so doing you will quickly identify the adjustments you need to make in order to advance your life plan. All of the questions in your self-assessment questionnaire may be summarised as follows:

> *'Are my daily activities producing my desired outcomes?' In other words, 'Is it working?'*

Personal Adjustments

At this point you must be very honest. If it is not working, why isn't it? But don't dwell on that question. Dwell rather on this question: 'What single adjustment can I make to my daily routine that will nigh guarantee my desired outcomes for the month ahead?'

If you are not seeing tangible results, use your Designer Life journal to identify inconsistencies, destructive patterns or strategic errors in your daily routine. Remember that where you are right now is the result of a direction you have been moving in over a period of time. Every action or failure to act constitutes a step in that direction. If you are constantly missing your targets then you should employ a change of strategy. This means tweaking your plan to include adjustments to your daily activities, whether by minuses (cutting out activities) or pluses (adding in activities). Adjustments are essential to the success of any plan. Never make your plan so rigid that there is no room for change. Be flexible!

Two of your self-assessment questions may be used for this purpose. One question is, 'Have you discovered any habits to break or form on this level? If so what?' and the other is 'What can you do to improve your performance on this level?'

Personal Acceleration

You can get to where you are going much quicker than you got to where you are. You got to where you are by taking significant steps in that direction over a period of time. However, most of those steps were taken subconsciously and inconsistently. The steps you are now taking in your dream direction are both conscious and consistent and should yield results more quickly.

Having conducted a self-assessment and made some personal adjustments, you are now back on track. Now that you are on the right track, you may accelerate. Personal acceleration comes when you require more from yourself and expect more from your program this month than you did last month. When seeking to accelerate you should shift gears by asking a new question. Instead of asking yourself each morning, 'What single thing can I do today that will take me one step closer to my desired destination?' you may now ask, 'What two things can I do today that will take me two steps closer to my desired destination?' and on and on until you are taking 4 or 5 steps a day in your dream direction. Accelerating means stepping up the pace, putting in more, expecting more out, and otherwise stretching your faith a little further.

Conclusion

The Triple A Technique works for personal achievement of whatever sort. When you start moving in your dream direction, towards your desired destination, this technique will regulate the process and ensure consistent progress. It is crucial to your life management strategy.

CHAPTER 7

Designing a Solution!

Solve Your Problems

Obstacles are those frightful things you see when you take your eyes off your goal.

Anonymous

CHAPTER 7

Designing a Solution!

Solve Your Problems

PROBLEMS ARE INEVITABLE. Even if you set clear goals, document your destiny and design your days, problems are still going to occur. This is not a bad thing because in fact your problems are essential to the success of your Designer Life plan. Apart from regular resistance, your muscles would simply pack up and die. When building muscles, controlled resistance is essential. We, who live by design, view our problems in exactly the same way. They are nothing more than a mental workout - a necessary exercise contributing to your overall mental health. As such, they are both essential and crucial to your personal development. For this reason, our life management system includes an effective strategy for dealing with problems.

So What Is The Problem?

A ***real problem*** is anything that hinders your progress towards a personal ideal or goal. This means that it must actually prevent you from moving forward or else it does not qualify as a problem.

Anything that threatens to hinder your progress is a ***potential problem.*** This means that it has the potential to stop you in your tracks but is not doing so as yet. Very often people react to potential problems as if they were present problems and bring their plans to a grinding halt even though nothing is actually preventing them from making progress.

A ***perceived problem*** is an impotent obstacle in your way. Impotent obstacles can be quite vocal but when examined prove to be powerless in the fight against your progress. I personally view impotent obstacles as cartoon characters, making lots of noise but possessing no power in the real world.

The rule is that real problems should be solved through remedial action. Potential problems should be arrested through preventative action. Perceived problems should be ignored and left behind.

5 Ineffective Reactions To A Problem:

1. **Shock:** There is no such thing as a full-proof plan. Anything can happen, and if anything can happen then something will happen. Don't be naive; anticipate it and predetermine your strategy for dealing with it.

2. **Ignore It:** Some people think that if they ignore a problem, it will eventually sort itself out and go away. This does happen with perceived problems but not with real or potential problems. The more you ignore them, the worse they become.

3. **Focus On It:** Some people get so completely embroiled in their problems until they lose sight of

their purpose, plan and progress to date. We must focus on solutions not problems. You must become solution-oriented and result-orientated, not problem and obstacle orientated.

4. **Fear:** Don't panic when a problem occurs. The fear alone will do more damage to your plans than the problem itself ever could. Fear is more dangerous than the thing you fear. Panic paralyses. Instead realise that there is a solution to this problem even if it is not evident right now. The fact that others have made it where you are going is living proof that it can be done. Those flags on the top of the mountain stand as proof that there is a way over this ridge.

5. **Surrender!** If failure is an option to you then problems will secure the death of your dreams. You must rule out the possibility of failure or retreat. You must never surrender to a problem. Never surrender to an obstacle. In the words of sir Winston Churchill, **'NEVER GIVE UP!'**

The Purpose Of Your Problem

There is a mysterious purpose for every problem you face. Nothing just happens. If you understand the purpose of your problems, you can harness the power of your problems. Problems are like pieces of power that come gift-wrapped in the strangest of ways. Life's gifts of power come securely wrapped up in a problem. Those with the dedication and patience to solve the problem will receive the power. Your worst problems may turn out to be your best friends because of what they bring out of you and because of what you become in the process of solving them. In this respect life is not working against you but for you. The problems it brings are never intended to destroy you but to develop you. If you understand what is going on, your problems will always serve your purposes. There are three unique purposes to your problems:

1. **To Squeeze Out Hidden Potential:** Hidden in you are the most phenomenal capabilities, concepts and creativity. Your inner genius will never be known until right kind of pressure forces and squeezes it out. When a baby is born, we know that it is more than a bundle of fun and that it is also a bundle of potential. We therefore create systems and institutions designed to get that

potential out. One such institution is school. For the child, school, homework, and maths are one big problem. But we don't feel sorry for him because we know that the pressure is squeezing out a genius. In the same way, your problems will bring out of you a new level of competence, concept and creativity that you would not have otherwise known.

2. **To Motivate You:** There are only two great motivators in life; they are pain and pleasure. Whenever we get lethargic, lazy, casual, and indifferent in our attitude towards progress, problems come along with so much pain attached that we are instantly motivated to get on with our plans and stop wasting time. In this way, problems can strengthen your resolve to achieve your goals and live your dreams. They may feed your faith, strengthen your beliefs and reinforce your personal philosophy. There are some moves you will never make in life until the pain of staying put outweighs the potential pain of taking action.

3. **To Educate You:** In the process of solving a problem, you will acquire new knowledge and skills. You will discover things you didn't know.

Often the problems will drive you to the library or to the Internet or to an expert to get information that you would otherwise not even have been interested in.

Design A Solution

Whenever a problem occurs, go to the Design a Solution page in your 90-Day Planner and work through the fields as follows:

1. **Define It:** In a nutshell what is the problem? Define it by just a one-liner or two-liner. Why? A problem defined is a problem half solved. Fifty percent of the problem is defining it.

2. **Describe It:** How exactly is it hindering your progress? What are its causes and effects and symptoms? Write just a few lines on this one. Why? Because it will become clear at this point exactly why you can't live with it, dither or procrastinate any further. You must get rid of it now.

3. **Detach It:** Put it in perspective. It is not your whole life. Don't become absorbed by it to the point of depression. Isolate it and celebrate all the good things happening in your life. Why? You will become fearful if you perceive the problem to be bigger than it is.

4. **Doubt It:** Don't doubt your destiny; doubt your doubts! Question the problem as though it were a person you did not trust or believe. Disbelieve its claims and refuse to listen to its propaganda. Why? Problems present themselves as invincible. You must not believe this but rather firmly maintain that there is a way through this.

5. **Determine Your Desired Outcome:** What do you want? How would you like this to be resolved? List three possible outcomes that you would be prepared to accept. List them as 1st, 2nd and 3rd choice. Why? Up until this point, your focus was the problem. When you decide what you want, you have effectively established a goal. You now know what you are aiming for and can create a pathway to it. You can now focus on the solution in a way that you could not before this point. The first step to getting where you want to go is

knowing where you want to go. This is the great turning point in your problem solving process and the master key to designing a solution.

6. **Design A Solution:** You are now ready to map out a number of routes to your chosen destinations. There will be a path that leads to your 1st, 2nd and 3rd choice. Instead of choosing one of these paths, employ the best features of all of them to get you where you want to go. Be flexible, not rigid. When designing your solution remember that there are only three ways to solve a problem. First is to move or eliminate it; explore that possibility. Second is to go around it; side step it in some way. To tweak your plans such that you can continue making progress in spite of it. Explore that possibility. Third is to buckle down and go through it. Go through the storm in the knowledge that this too will pass. That may be the answer.

7. **Deal With It:** Designing a solution does not deal with the problem. Implementing your solution does.

8. **Document It:** Monitor your progress using your journal. In days to come it will be a great source of inspiration and education for you and others.

CHAPTER 8

Conditioning Yourself to Win

Peak-Performance Conditioning!

The men who succeed are the efficient few. They are the few who have the ambition and willpower to develop themselves.

Herbert N. Casson

CHAPTER 8

Conditioning Yourself to Win

Peak-Performance Conditioning!

PEAK PERFORMANCE REQUIRES a peak state. Your level of mental and physical fitness will impact your plans and progress for better or worse. The fitness factor cannot be ignored. It is crucial to the success of your mission for three reasons:

1. True success is not the one hundred meter sprint but rather the cross-country marathon. It requires true stamina to keep going across the rugged and

unpredictable terrain and through the adverse weather that may strike at any moment. Likewise, it requires both mental and physical stamina to proceed with your life plan in the face of adverse circumstances, life challenges, disappointments and change. Stamina is not a gift. It is a state and condition that can be developed by anyone through regular exercise.

2. The psychosomatic relationship means that your state of mind will affect your physical competence and your physical condition will affect your state of mind. Health is a holistic state. Physical ailments often have psychological roots and vice-versa.

3. Your mental and physical condition is effectively your state. A poor state equals a poor performance. A poor performance equals under achievement. The difference between a poor state and a peak state is your daily routine. The person in peak state does things on a daily basis that the person in a poor state does not. Likewise the person in a poor state does things on a daily basis that people in peak state do not. If you do the things on a daily basis that peak performers do,

you will become a peak performer yourself and thus optimise your level of achievement.

For these reasons, it is essential that you start each day with a set of exercises designed to condition you for a successful day and to develop that peak state for peak performance and lifelong success.

Daily Success Conditioning!

Your daily performance conditioning should take place first thing in the morning before your day begins. This will mean getting up a little earlier than usual. The routine may take anywhere from 15 minutes to one hour and should include the following exercises:

1. **Spiritual Exercises:** These may include, prayer, thanksgiving, Bible reading, and mediation on spiritual things. If you start the day with God, you can end the day with grace.

2. **Physical Exercises:** These include stretching, deep breathing for improved circulation, cardiovascular exercise (e.g. walking, running, skipping,

swimming, cycling), and taking your vitamins and minerals, etc.

3. **Mental Exercises:** These include reading your five-year plan, completing your day planner, idealising your future, memorising a quote, counting your blessings, reviewing your 90-day plan, positive confessions and one-step creativity.

4. **Social Exercises:** Chose three people to touch, surprise and bless today. Think of ways to reinforce and strengthen your most valuable relationships.

Of course, you cannot do all of these things every day but you should insure that you touch each category. Some of these exercises overlap. This is a good idea. You should find ways of combining each category, e.g. strategic with mental and spiritual with social or physical with mental and strategic with spiritual and social. The end result should be 15 minutes to one hour of exercises that prepare you for the day and condition you for life.

You should take your health and fitness seriously if you intend to enjoy the future. Join a health club, eat nutritious and natural foods, drink plenty of water, get plenty of exercise and rest well.

Conclusion

The Designer Life System can only regulate the outcomes of your days, months and years if you use the technologies habitually. To do so, you must develop the master habit of Living By Design. Advancing your five-year plan in 90-day increments using the 90-day planner and the 90-day journal can all become an effortless way of life if you stick it through for 90 days.

Set 12 strategic goals for the next 90 days. Fill out your 90-day planner (available from Designer Life Technologies Inc. at www.waynemalcolm.com). Fill out your journal every day for 90 days. Conduct a personal assessment every 30 days, use the problem solver when you run into problems, condition yourself for peak performance daily...do it, do it, do it...design your new life and live it now!

Getting from where you've been to where you belong is not rocket science. It is the result of a simple yet proven formula for success. The science of success says that if you apply the laws of success to your goals, you will achieve them. The laws are causes and success is the predictabsle result of applying those laws. Regardless of your colour or creed you can achieve your goals, live your dreams and get maximum results in every area of your life.

Take action and do it now!

Additional Reading:

The Holy Bible

7 Strategies for Wealth and Happiness
Jim Rohn

Focal Point
Brian Tracy

It's Not Over Until You Win
Les Brown

It Only Takes Everything You've Got
Julio Melara

The Success Journey
John Maxwell

Think and Grow Rich
Napolean Hill